Exploring Maths

Colour in a sweet when you complete a page.

Compiled by John Drinkwater
Illustrated by Mike Gordon

Ladybird Books

Counting to 10

Here are the numbers from 0 to 10.

0	1	2	3	4	5	6	7	8	9	10
zero	one	two	three	four	five	six	seven	eight	nine	ten

These children are all wearing party hats.

Colour the hats.

Give two children red hats.

Give three children green hats.

Give the rest blue hats.

Complete the sentences by filling in the missing number. The first one has been done for you.

There are [2] red hats.

There are [3] green hats.

There are [5] blue hats.

There are [10] hats altogether.

There are [3] more blue hats than red hats.

Order

Ten animals decided to have a race. Fill in the table below to show their position.

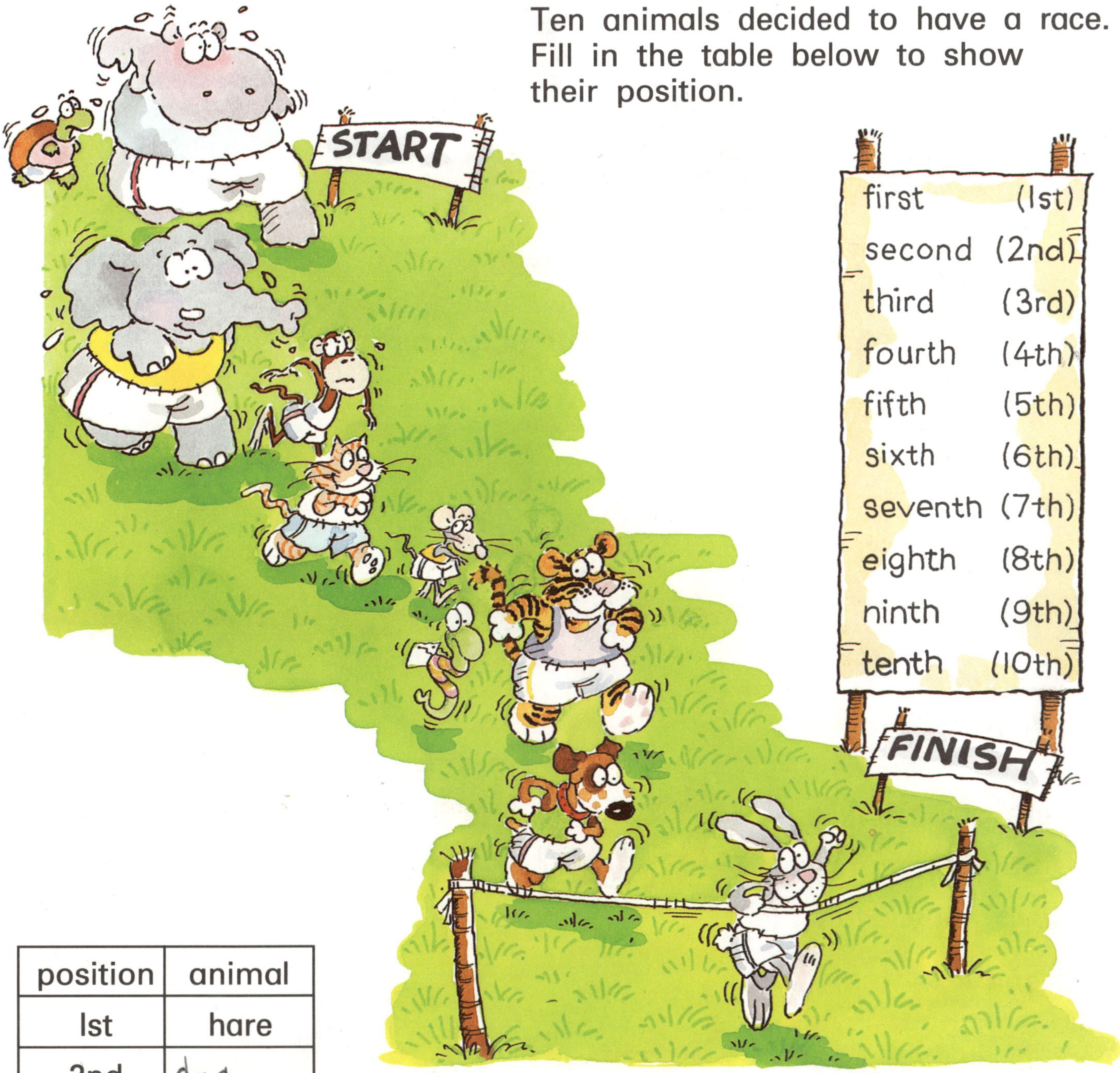

START
first (1st)
second (2nd)
third (3rd)
fourth (4th)
fifth (5th)
sixth (6th)
seventh (7th)
eighth (8th)
ninth (9th)
tenth (10th)
FINISH

position	animal
1st	hare
2nd	dog.
third	tiger
4th	snake.
Fifth.	mouse
sixth.	cat
7th	monkey
eighth	elephant
ninth.	hippo
10th	snail

Draw the winners with their medals.

first
second
third

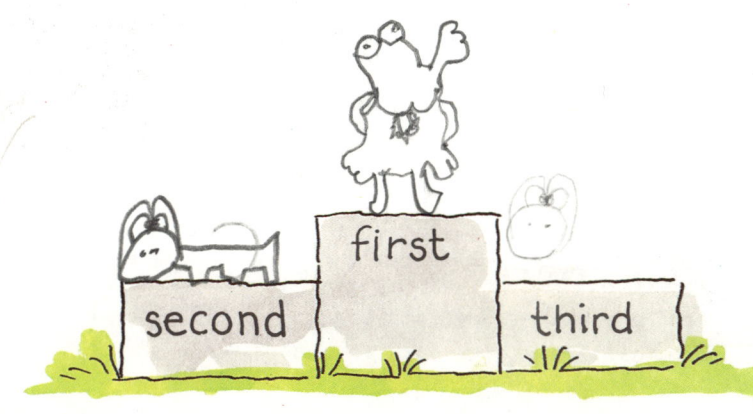

Adding

Here are four hedgehogs.
Draw two more.

How many altogether? Write your answer in the box.

4 and 2 → [6] ✓

Here are two parrots.
Draw three more.

How many altogether?

2 and 3 → [5] ✓

Here are six flags.
Draw one more.
How many altogether?

6 and 1 → [7] ✓

Here are five dogs.
Draw four more.
How many altogether?

5 and 4 → [9] ✓

When we add on, we use the + sign.

Four rabbits add three more rabbits is seven rabbits.

This can be written as a sum:
4 + 3 = 7

= is the sign for equals.

Can you add these?

Write your answer in the boxes below.

2 cows add on 4 cows = 6

2 + 4 = 6

6 clowns add on 2 clowns = 8

6 + 2 = 8

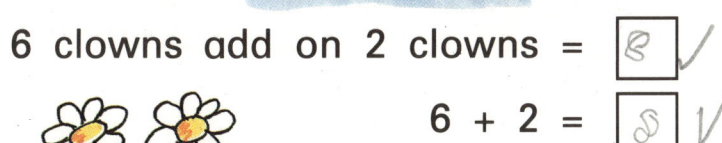

7 flowers add on 2 flowers = 9

7 + 2 = 9

Write the answer in the box.

8 + 2 = 10

1 + 9 = 10

3 + 1 = 4

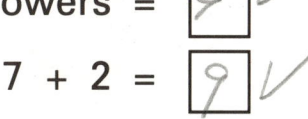

6 + 4 = 10

2 + 5 = 7

4 + 3 = 7

Number pairs to 10

Draw petals on the flowers so each flower has 10 petals.

Write the number of petals you have drawn in the box to complete the number pairs to 10.

10 + [0] = 10 ✓

9 + [19] = 10 ✓

8 + [18] = 10 ✓

7 + [17] = 10 ✓

6 + [16] = 10 ✓

5 + [15] = 10 ✓

4 + [14] = 10 ✓

3 + [13] = 10 ✓

2 + [12] = 10 ✓

1 + [11] = 10 ✓

0 + [10] = 10 ✓

It is very important that you know the number pairs to 10.

Get an adult to check your work, then learn all the number pairs to 10.

Shapes

Here are some shapes.

triangles   circles

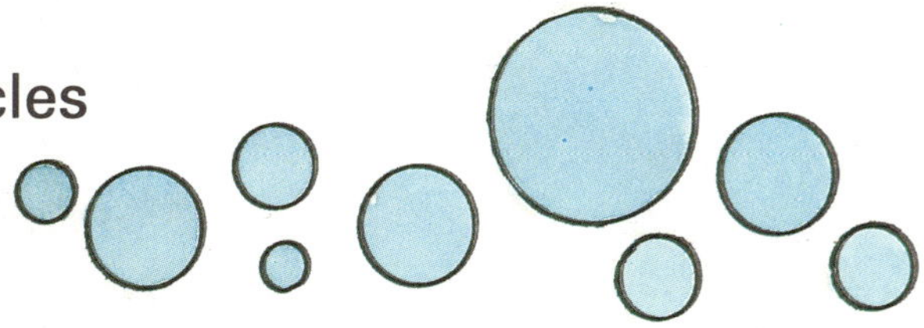

squares    pentagons

rectangles 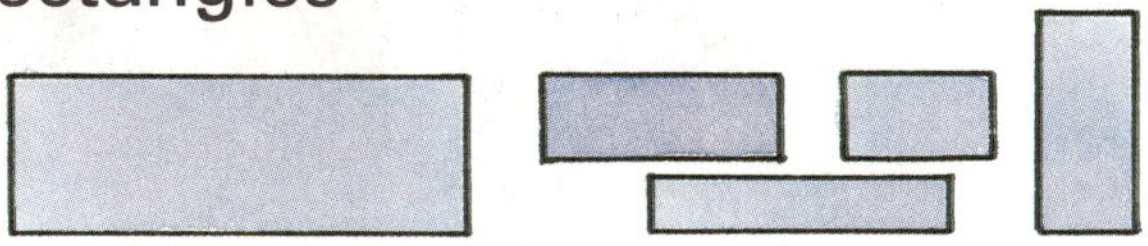   hexagons

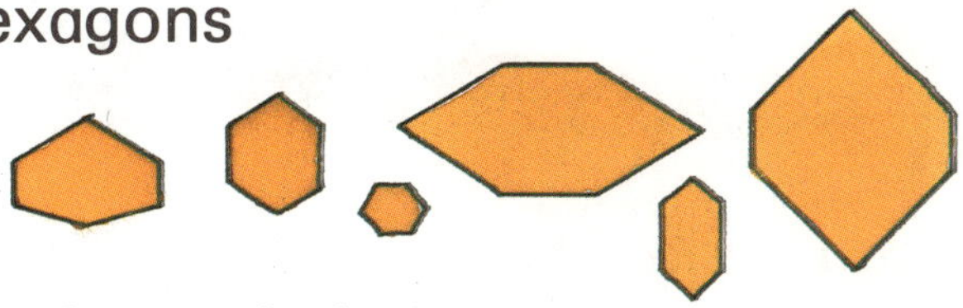

Count the sides. Write the answer in each box.

Triangles have [3] sides.   Pentagons have [5] sides.

Squares have [4] sides.   Hexagons have [6] sides.

Rectangles have [4] sides.

There is a picture hidden below. Find it by colouring all the segments that have a triangle inside.

Subtraction

Here are 6 eggs.

The farmer **takes away** 3 eggs.

There are
3 eggs left.

We can write this as a sum: 6 − 3 = 3

Complete these sums by writing the correct number in the box.

10 − 4 = 6

7 − 2 = 5

8 − 5 = 3

5 − 1 = 4

9 − 3 = 6

Counting back

Here is the number line from 1 to 20.

0 1 2 3 4 5 6 7 8 9 10 11 12 13 14 15 16 17 18 19 20

If you start on 20 and count back 2 you get to 18.

Use the number line to continue counting back in 2s.

20 → 18 → 16 → 14 → 12 → 10

Start on 18 and count back in 3s.

18 → 15 → 10 → 7 → 4 → 3

Start on 20 and count back in 4s.

20 → 16 → 12 → 8 → 3 → 0

Match the spaceships to the planets.

Using a ruler

Join the two red dots by drawing a straight line between them using a ruler.

Remember to hold the ruler still.

Now use your ruler to measure the line. Write your answer in the box.

*Make sure you line up the **start** of your ruler with the left hand dot.*

The line measures ☐ centimetres.

I measured the line, too. It measures 8 centimetres.

I measured the lines below but got my answers muddled up.

Can you help by measuring the lines and matching them to the correct answers?

The first one has been done for you.

a.
b.
c.
d.
e.
f.

Answers

2 centimetres

7 centimetres

9 centimetres

6 centimetres

4 centimetres

3 centimetres

Why not try measuring things in your home, such as tables or doors?

Function machines

The machine below is a function machine.
If you put a number in it the machine changes the number.
The input number is changed into a different output number.

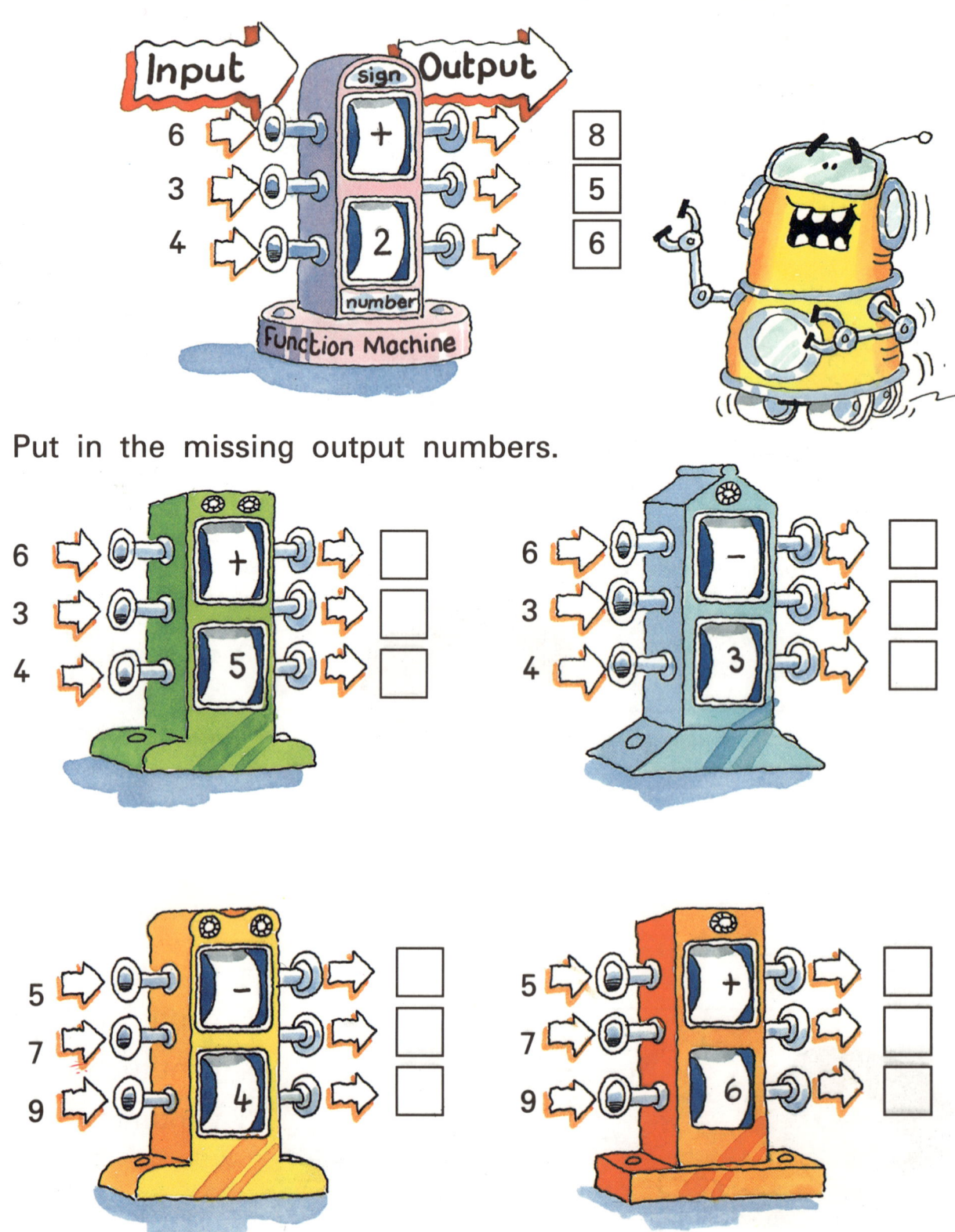

Put in the missing output numbers.

This function machine adds 3 to each input number.

Some signs and numbers have been left off these machines. Complete by filling in the boxes.

Write the input and output number of these machines.

Multiplication

Here are 2 octopuses. Each octopus has eight legs.
How many legs altogether?

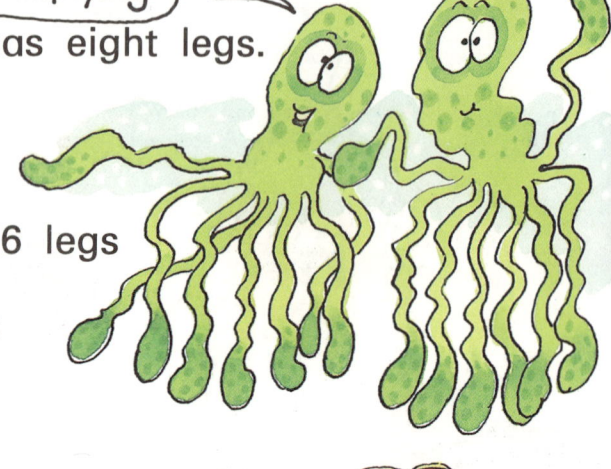

There are **2 sets of 8 legs** or 2(8) = 16 legs

We usually write these sums like this:

2 × 8 = 16

These are **multiplication** sums.

Complete the following:

Here are 4 pairs of socks.
How many socks altogether?

| 4 | × | 2 | = | 8 |

Here are 3 boys. Each boy has 10 toes.
How many toes altogether?

| 3 | × | 10 | = | 30 |

Here are 5 jackets. Each jacket has 4 buttons.
How many buttons altogether?

| 5 | × | 4 | = | 20 |

Here are 3 ladybirds. Each ladybird has 6 legs.
How many legs altogether?

| 3 | × | 6 | = | 18 |

Here are 3 flags. Each flag has 5 stars.
How many stars altogether?

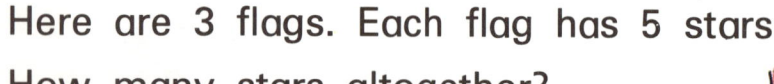

| 3 | × | 5 | = | 15 |

Each bicycle has 2 wheels.

How many wheels on 1 bicycle?

1 × 2 = 2

How many wheels on 2 bicycles?

2 × 2 = 4

How many wheels on 3 bicycles?

3 × 2 = 6

How many wheels on 4 bicycles?

4 × 2 = 8

Each frog has 4 spots.

How many spots on 1 frog?

1 × 4 = 4

How many spots on 2 frogs?

2 × 4 = 8

How many spots on 3 frogs?

3 × 4 = 12

How many spots on 4 frogs?

4 × 4 = 16

Draw a line to join each balloon to the correct clown.

15

Division

Here are 6 cakes. If they were shared equally between 2 friends, how many would each friend get?

Each friend would get 3 cakes.

This can be written as a sum:

6 cakes shared between 2 friends = 3 cakes

6 ÷ 2 = 3

÷ is the sign for sharing or dividing.

Share these arrows equally between the two targets.
How many arrows in each target?

10 ÷ 2 = 5

Share these eggs equally between the five boxes.
How many eggs in each box?

15 ÷ 5 = ☐

Divide these beads equally between the four necklaces.
How many beads on each necklace?

24 ÷ 4 = ☐

Divide these buttons equally between the three shirts.
How many buttons on each shirt?

24 ÷ 3 = ☐

Now try these. You may like to use real objects, such as buttons or counters, to help you.

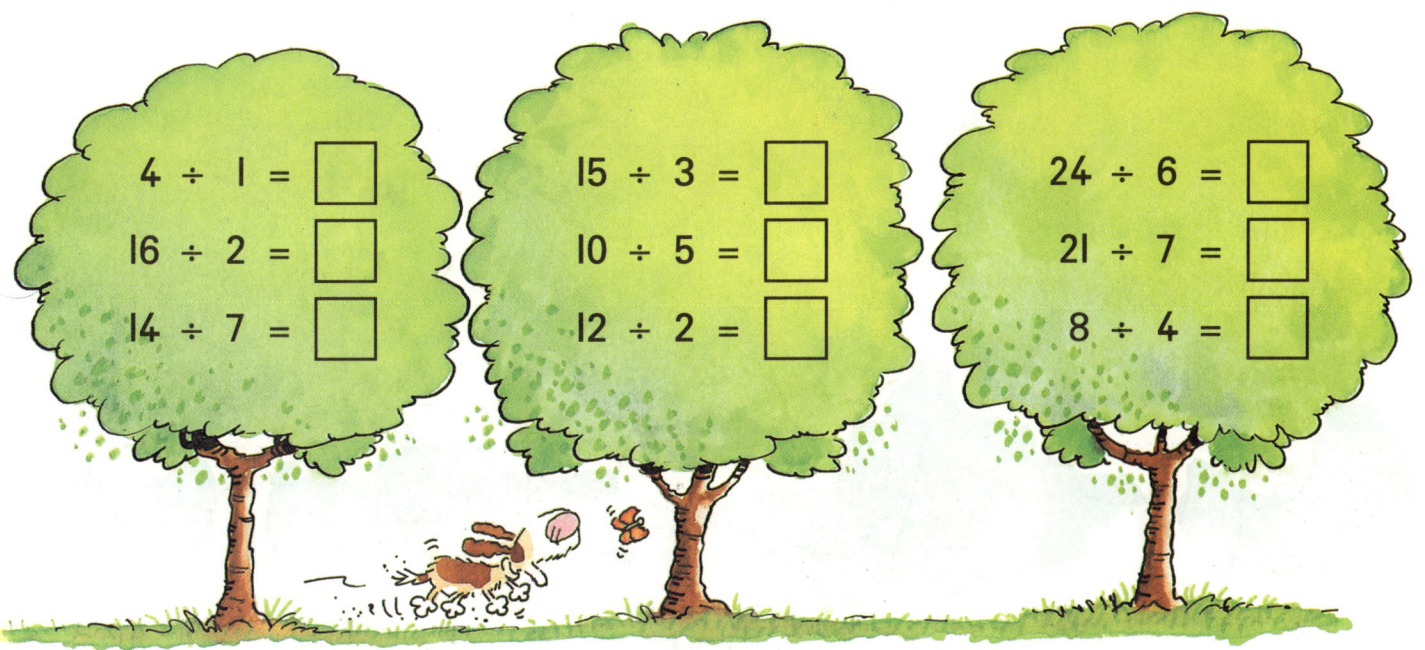

4 ÷ 1 = ☐
16 ÷ 2 = ☐
14 ÷ 7 = ☐
15 ÷ 3 = ☐
10 ÷ 5 = ☐
12 ÷ 2 = ☐
24 ÷ 6 = ☐
21 ÷ 7 = ☐
8 ÷ 4 = ☐

Which fish goes into which net?

Draw a line to join each fish to the correct net.

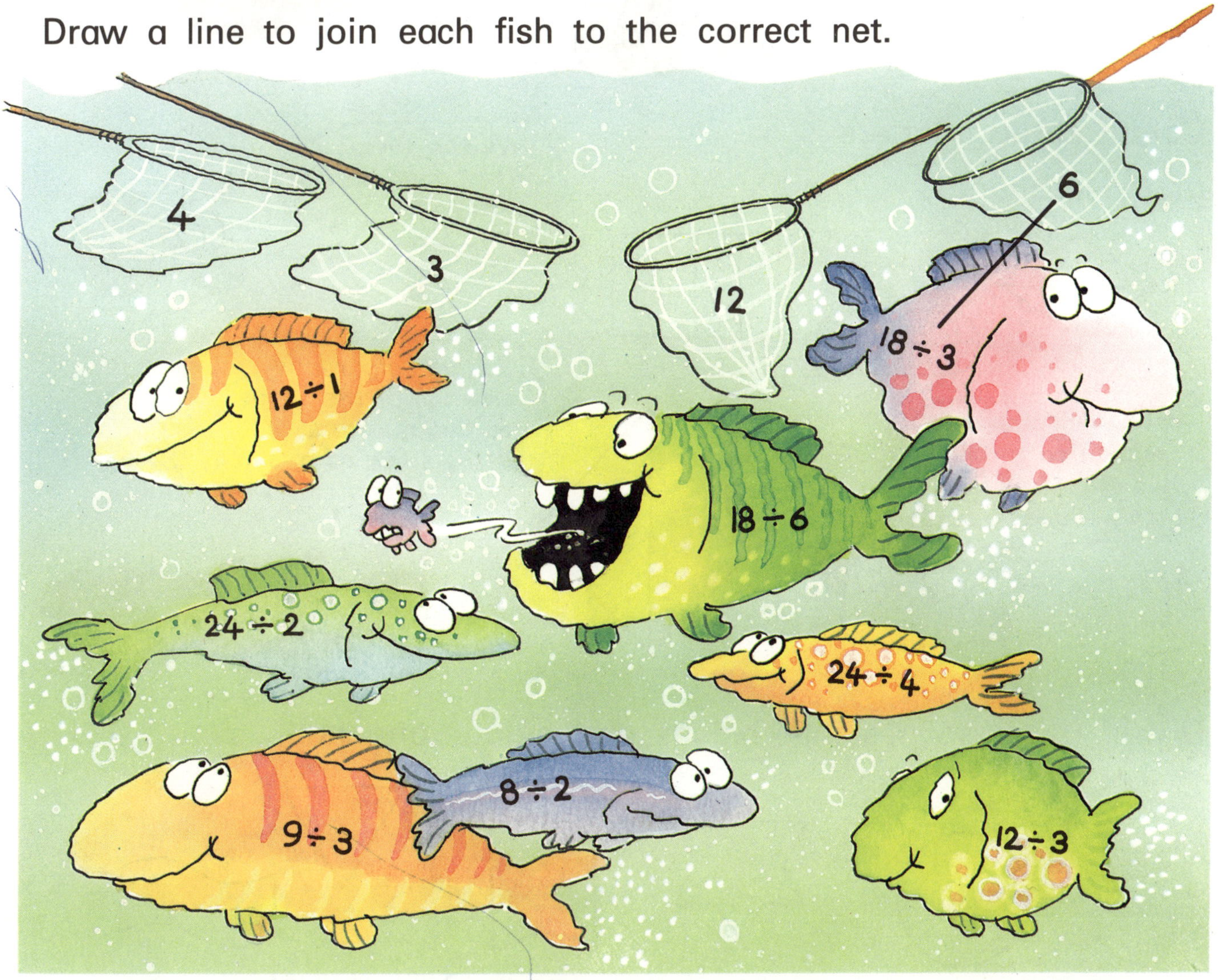
4
3
12
6
18÷3
12÷1
18÷6
24÷2
24÷4
8÷2
9÷3
12÷3

Fractions

This circle has been divided into 4 equal parts.

Each part is called a **quarter**.

The sign for a quarter is $\frac{1}{4}$.

$\frac{1}{4}$ part equal parts

Colour a quarter of each shape.

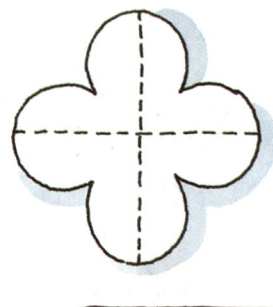
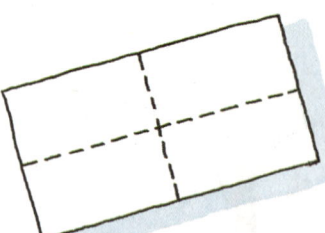
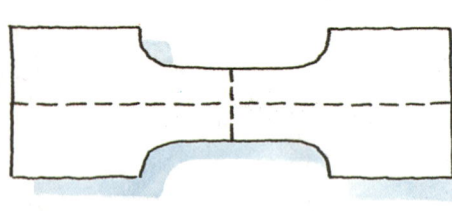

I've coloured three quarters of this leaf.

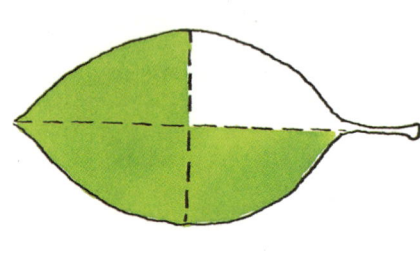

Colour three quarters of these shapes.

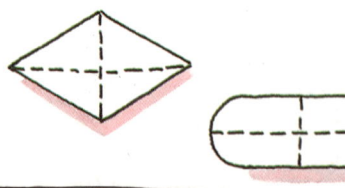

We can write three quarters like this: $\frac{3}{4}$.

Look what happens when I colour two quarters of this shape.

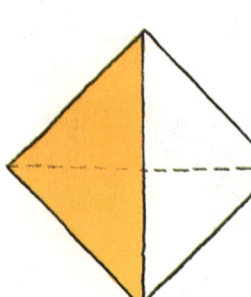

You've coloured one half of the shape, so two quarters is the same as one half!

Divide these shapes into halves and colour one half.

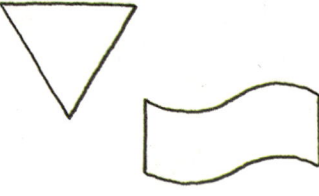

Tens and units

Count the blocks.

There are 3 groups of 10 [3] tens.

There are 7 single blocks [7] units.

Count the numbers of tens and units. Fill in the boxes.

[1] tens [2] units

[ ] tens [ ] units

[ ] tens [ ] units

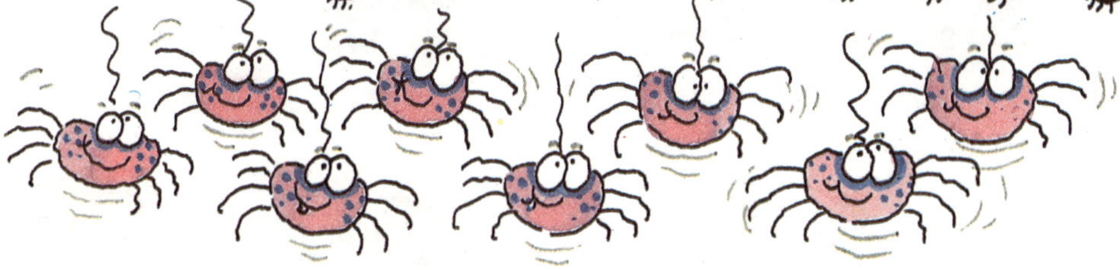

[ ] tens [ ] units

How many tens in these numbers?

76 [7] tens   50 [ ] tens

92 [ ] tens   42 [ ] tens

13 [ ] tens   29 [ ] tens

How many units in these numbers?

38 [8] units   96 [ ] units

84 [ ] units   27 [ ] units

60 [ ] units   10 [ ] units

Fill in the missing numbers in the hundred square below.

1	2		4			7	8		
		13	14	15			18		
21	22			25	26			29	
		33				37	38	39	40
41			44		46		48	49	
	52	53		55	56	57			60
61			64	65		67	68		
71	72				76	77		79	
	82	83		85			87		90
91			94		96			98	99	100

Look at the numbers below. Start at 2 and show how far you can count in twos. Join the numbers using red arrows. Your number square can help you.

Start at 18 and show how far you can count in threes. Join the numbers using blue arrows.

Start at 5 and show how far you can count in fives. Join the numbers using green arrows.

Multiplication triangles

Look at this multiplication triangle.

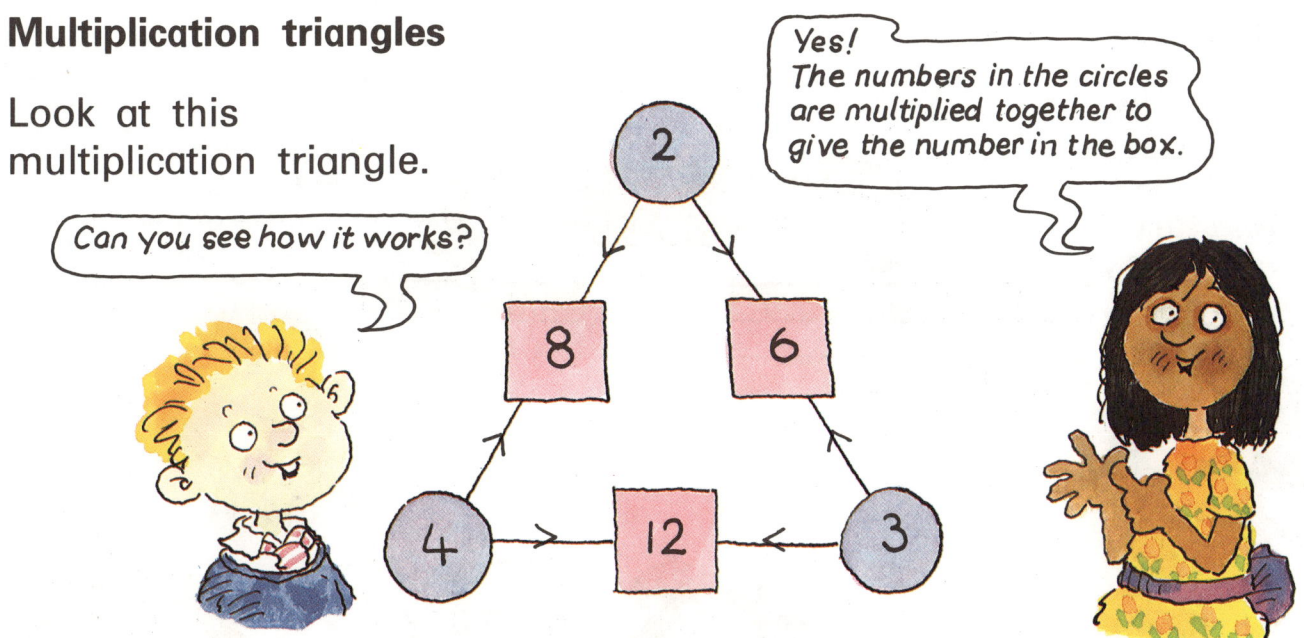

Complete these multiplication triangles by writing the missing numbers in the boxes.

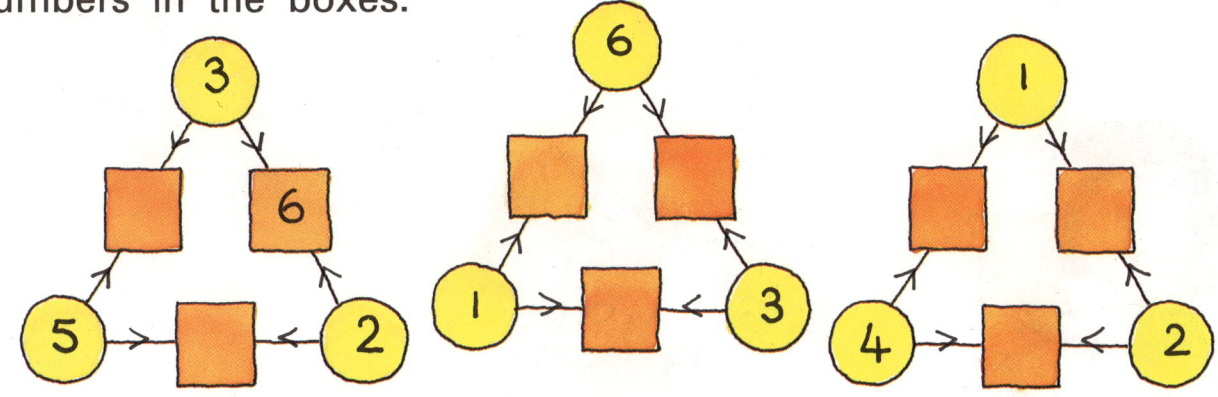

These are more difficult. Complete by writing the missing numbers in the circles and squares.

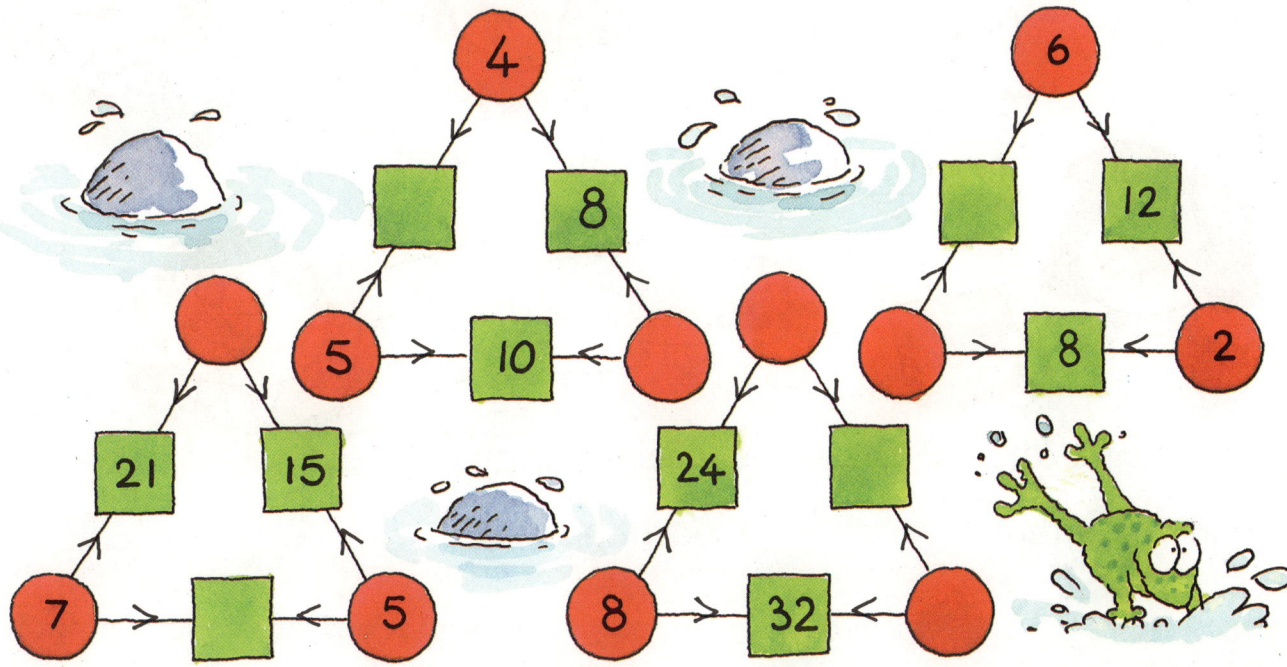

Greater than, less than

Look at this number:

Who has the greater (bigger) number?

First look at the tens digits.

7 is greater than 5, so 72 is greater than 53.

What if the tens digits are the same?

Look at the units digits.

4 is greater than 3, so 44 is greater than 43.

Circle the greater number in each pair.

| 62 | 24 | 32 | 29 | 22 | 41 | 12 | 16 |
| 91 | 77 | 17 | 63 | 31 | 32 | 15 | 51 |

When we say 'is greater than' we can use a symbol like this >.

When we say 'is less than' we can use a symbol like this <.

Complete:

17 > 12   19   39   51   61   13   31

33   42   7   4   26   22   73   37

Adding made easy

Here are three sums.

30 + 7 = 37

20 + 1 = 21

37 + 21 = 58

We can make hard sums much easier to do.
Look at this sum.

26 + 43

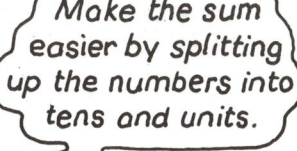

20 + 6 + 40 + 3

20 + 40 + 6 + 3 = 60 + 6 + 3

60 + 6 + 3 = 60 + 9

The answer is 69.

See if you can do the same with these sums.

23 + 46 = 20 + [3] + 40 + [ ]

= 60 + [ ] + [ ]

= 60 + [ ] = [ ]

37 + 22 = [ ] + 7 + [ ] + 2

= [ ] + [ ] + [ ]

= [ ] + [ ] = [ ]

56 + 21 = [ ] + [ ] + [ ] + [ ]

= [ ] + [ ] + [ ]

= [ ] + [ ] = [ ]

73 + 24 = [ ] + [ ] + [ ] + [ ]

= [ ] + [ ] + [ ]

= [ ] + [ ] = [ ]

15 + 62 = [60] + [ ] + [ ] + [ ]

= [ ] + [ ] + [ ]

= [ ] + [ ] = [ ]

I have given you some help to begin with.

Well done! You can now do difficult sums!